WHISPERS
IN AFRICA

Josiah F. Joekai Jr.

FORTE
PUBLISHING
IDEAS! WORDS! BOOKS! RESULTS!

First Published in 2016
Published by:
FORTE Publications
#12 Ashmun Street
Snapper Hill
Monrovia, Liberia

FORTE Publishing
7202 Tavenner Lane
208 Alexandria
VA, 22306

FORTE Press
76 Sarasit Road
Ban Pong, 70110
Ratchaburi, Thailand

http://fortepublishing.wix.com/fppp

Printed in the United States of America

ISBN-10: 0-9946308-0-8
ISBN-13: 978-0-9946308-0-3

Dedication

Whispers in Africa

is dedicated
to all the great African and
Pan Africanist leaders.
From the age old beginnings of
Dr. Edward W. Blyden, Alexander Crumwell, to the
much recent voices of presidents Kwame Nkrumah,
William R. Tolbert, Nelson Mandela, Thomas Sankara,
Sekou Toure, Daniel Moi, the towering Steven Beko
and Patrice Lumumba, and the countless others
who sought and spoke the truth.

Your whispers and shouts
Fell not on deaf ears.
Thank you for planting
The seeds.

Now, we water
Nurture and
Realize
the dream

Table of Contents

Acknowledgement

Firstly I wish to acknowledge God's eternal grace and mercy that he continues to grant me bountifully. It is this sanctification that has brought me this far in my life journey, especially at this point of the publication of my 4th book. I am grateful to God for the opportunity granted me to contribute meaningfully to the education of my fellow compatriots.

Secondly, my sincere gratitude goes to one of my mentors, the Director of the Kofi Annan Institute for Conflict Transformation at the University of Liberia, Prof. T. Debey Sayndee for his professional guidance in the writing process. My appreciation goes to all academicians and other professional colleagues who one way or the other contributed to the undertaking and completion of this book.

Finally, I would like to express my thanks and appreciation to the **FORTE** Publications for the professional manner in which it was published. Indeed, it has the quality it deserves.

Section I

WHISPERS IN AFRICA

Section I

The poems in this section are of general nature.
They cover a range of contemporary issues as
well as personal issues.

Incredible Africa

Africa, beauty abashed in poverty
striking in the splendor of diversity
rich cultures, religions and skin tones
Africa, unmatched climate,
Enviable rain forests
Exotic species of all kinds
A testimony of bursting spectrum

Africa, naturally endowed with resources
Gold, diamond, iron ore,
Uranium, oil and bauxite
Incredibly, you sink in poverty

Africa, last among equals
Quality of life, one so unbearable
Justice and equality, still illusive
Education and health care, appalling
Infrastructure and housing, inacceptable
Jobs and food production, unlikely
Preyed on by brutal and selfish dictators
Africa, a victim of circumstances

Africa, are you awake?
Your sons and daughters wallop in poverty
As slum dwellers and poor laborers
Suffering mothers and children languish

But warlords and smugglers steal your wealth
Stashing away millions and billions
To invest in western economies
And brutes and shady elites are rewarded
Oh Africa, you're a looter's paradise

Oh my Africa, what a tragedy?
Plagued by illiteracy, disease,
Religious and ethnic conflicts;
Catastrophe and chaos engulf you
Underdeveloped and suffering as
The poor gets poorer, rich gets richer
Africa, you're indeed incredible

"Incredible Africa" is a true reflection of the author's views on Africa as an incredible continent. His opinion is based on the paradoxical reality that the continent is naturally endowed but yet the poorest. He tries to present a clearer picture of the causes of Africa's impoverishment and the consequences thereof citing illiteracy and bad governance reflective of uneven distribution of resources and shady investments with huge rewards for the maintenance of status quos to the disadvantage of the majority of people. He equates Africa to "Looters' Paradise" signifying the extent to which the continent has been exploited and drained by its own sons and daughters who then invest particularly in the western world. The author believes that Africa is underdeveloped due to the actions and inactions of Africans themselves. Thus, no need for blame shifting.

Under my Father's Kola Tree

My father's kola tree is a symbol of a great culture.
With large branches and evergreen leaves
it produces nuts throughout the year.
It accommodates everyone, men, women, children
the old and young, the weary and the wise.
It towers majestically overlooking the St. Paul River
edging the horizon above the distant forest
My Father's Kola Tree is on the edge of our village,
Toukorbah, the origin of Kpelle hospitality,
Toukorbah, the birthplace of Kpelle generosity
Toukorbah, the homeland of Kpelle ethnicity

My Father's Kola Tree protects us.
It absorbs the unfading sunrays
offering a shade to rest and think
as the natural breeze wheezes in
from across the St. Paul River
whilst hosts birds sing sweet melodies
and squirrels and lizards pursue their goals
Oh, how I cherish my father's kola tree

Under my Father's Kola Tree, we play and
we runabout without limits; we marvel at God's
wonderful creation; we watch the gushing estuaries
of the St. Paul's snaking on its watery path from
uphill; we hear echoes of distant forest creatures
and the calmness of it all gives us belongingness.
Yes, under my Father's Kola Tree, there's harmony

Under my Father's Kola Tree
when the sky swallows up the sun,
our village elders proudly assemble.
They divide kola nuts and drink palm wine
they trade jokes, they laugh and tease
they share memories and enjoy the ambiance

Ah, they talk palavers and serious things.
Oh yes, they decide the fate of our village
promoting peace, love and unity or
advocating war, revenge and justice
many many things happen right here.
Ah, under My Father's Kola Tree....

Under My Father's Kola Tree,
there is place for everyone
for whoever from wherever;
Even travelers from nearby villages
transit under My Father's Kola Tree
sharing the nuts of my father's kola tree
drinking from the calm water of the creek
enjoying the gentle breeze from across the river
Oh under my father's kola tree
There is hope and there is life.

The poem "Under my Father's Kola Tree" is an appreciation of African tradition symbolic of a culture unique to the continent.

In Africa, kola is an endearing and valuable product, which represents love, peace and unity in addition to having a commercial value. In short, the adage "kola brings life" summarizes its significance in promoting coherence and peaceful co-existence among peoples of different cultures and traditions. Kola is a bridge that unites and build relationships. In essence, the tree that produces kola is not ordinary. It is a place that provides a platform for settling disputes, merry making, performing rites, transiting and making crucial decisions for families and communities.

Truly, in my village stands an old kola tree with a long standing and rich history of being a beacon of hope for communities on both sides of the St. Paul River between Liberia and Guinea in the north. It is forbidden to cut it down except by consensus. It is an undeniable heritage that is upheld by its surrounding communities and everyone including me is obliged to pay homage to it as reflected by this poem. Indeed, I love my father's kola tree.

In My Grandma's Custody

In my grandma's house, we are
greeted by early morning birds
anchored on branches of an old almond tree.
They sing the unchangeable choruses
with their unpleasant chirpings gnawing
deep into our ears, ceaselessly echoing,
and annoyingly keeping us awake.
Thus, they announce the morning

Through a single, narrow opened window
and along walls made of brown caked earth,
hot wheeling air ventilates the old clay house.
'though confining and discomforting in summer
But it blows the freshness of the African morning
Loaded with spices, homemade cuisines and dust

At my grandma's, there's a custody of certainty
freedom is measured and discipline dispensed
we are both embellished with our attributes.
Where I am bold, acrobatic and impatient
my grandma is stern, inflexible and patient
where I fuss and frown; complain or whine
My grandma simply smiles and giggles

Although my grandma is oft unpredictable
in grandma's custody, everything is possible
I can be all I want. In grandma's care I am secured

The poem reflects the general upbringing of many African children, which rest with their grandparents particularly, grandmothers. Brought up by his grandma during difficult times, the author reflects on some of the challenges young or teen African families faced in caring for their children.

Education sojourns in most cases are shattered, hopes and aspirations for better life remain bleak and obviously hopeless future sets in. Little Joe was one of such kid but very lucky that his grandmother's relationship with American Peace Corps was extended to him indirectly.

In his grandmother's two-room clay house, his dad and mommy who were junior secondary school students shared one of the two rooms and he and his grandmother share the other.

Spending the day in confinement with his grandmother while his parents were in school was an experience that the typical African referred to as "bitter-sweet".

Meaning there were rosy and sour moments. Even with those moments, he was the best grandson for his rewards were consistent and appreciated by him.

Unspeakable Silence

Silence, dead silence; the once tender air,
now pungent with decay, soared aimlessly.
The lights flickered but abruptly aborted
the streets around, completely deserted.
And suddenly everyone screamed hopelessly
fumbling about in your notorious paradise
where guns and machetes brutally rule
where they murder indiscriminately
Oh! Your reign was awful

You silent monster, brutally
brandishing your killer machines to-
destroy relationships and families
break cultures and traditions
murder innocent children
they were cruel to the helpless
were ruthless to the harmless
merciless to the homeless
They were beasts without hearts

Silence borne out of fear, engulfs us
tiny whispers and gestures echo
we're horrified in makeshift shelters
we are forced to see dreadful things
we weep and sob silently Oo...oh oh!
No! Oh! Ayee... yet in the distance, we hear
echoes of gunfire and gnashing of daggers
and there's more bloodshed and chaos.

The atmosphere is gloomy
even the air is still as scattered around
in polls of blood, marked with deep cuts
and gushing wounds, lie dead bodies
that embraced their butchers' slashes.
They confront cold-blooded monsters
who in their shameful misled prowess
snubbed the truth of their consciences
and did unspeakable evil deeds.

Silence! Dead silence screams loudly.
It resonates, demanding but one thing-
Justice. But what it so seeks was denied

"Unspeakable Silence" reflects the circle of brutality and mayhem that have often beset African societies in general. Civil wars, terrorism and secret killings have inundated Africa. North, South, East, West and Central regions of the continent have experienced waves of human catastrophes beyond imagination. Sadly, no enemies. Africa is simply self-destroying. Justice is either in short supply or non-existent for the most part. "Unspeakable Silence" summarizes this uncivilized and vicious culture that has engendered fear and silence in yet the far-more remotest (Underdeveloped) continent.

My Piassava Wine

It comes naturally fermented
distilled not, diluted, no....
bottled not, wrapped, no...
not even unduly processed
From god to man, you're given
My piassava wine, the African wine

Creamy, milky and pasty,
you are very refreshing.
Tapped from wild piassava trees,
grown along swamps, streams and creeks
my piassava wine is unique in its own way.

Mornings and evenings all across Africa
oh yes, from north to south; the east to west
men and women queue along paths or squares
impatiently, they wait telling stories and giggling
they inspire; they transpire; oh they are on fire
whenever bottles, jugs and calabashes are served

Yes, my piassava wine
kindled amidst confusion
served with smiles, excitingly,
stimulates communal farmers.
It inspires dowry rituals.
Oh, what a tradition?
My piassava wine, the African wine

"My Piassava Wine" is the author's realistic reflection of the uniqueness of the African wine, piassava wine. Grown in Africa, piassava or palm trees produce wine that is found across the African continent.

Although not very common to northern Africa, but it is a wine very common to east, west, central and south African societies.

This unique wine has proven to be a stimulant, source of excitement, motivation and inspiration for cultural and traditional rites such as dowry, child naming, conflict resolution and unifying ceremonies.

As a true African, the author finds it befitting to herald the significance of the African wine, which in his opinion is a symbol of African tradition that the rest of the world must come to understand.

The Courage to Love

At times, we are captured
emotionally by affection
in an uncontrollable feeling.
It consumes us innately
deep-down within beings
It is invisible, it is called love
We all have the courage to love

When it strikes, everyone falls prey to it
the young, the old; the abled and disabled
the poor, rich, the dejected... we all crave love.
Indeed, everyone has the courage to love.

Love is contagious and dynamic.
Love affects every soul that lives.
Love infests every heart that beats.
Love brightens each face that frowns.
Wonderfully unraveling its many lines.

In good times or bad times, love *is.*
Love is kind, sweet and peaceful.
Oh Love is fair, just and cheerful.
Love is humble and understanding.
It is not always easy nor painless.
Everyone has the courage to love

Amazingly, love exists not in isolation;
not in a vacuum, nor in an empty space
but throughout the cosmos it binds.
Love is deeply rooted in our hearts
carried within our inner beings
but enslaved by our consciences.
When wrong, it has consequences
When right, it is a blissful heaven

As carriers and agents of love
We are victims of fear,
victims of pain and
victims of disaster
When love is raided, we are weakened.
Arrogance, hate, and deceit invade our hearts
we are unable to face our raider,
We lack the courage to confront!

When trust and confidence
are mere subjects of the lips
hopelessness and despair are alternatives.
But when love rekindles, we regain strength.
We are revived; we are resuscitated; we're alive.
Oh yes, we become fearless and resolute
For love heals, reunites and transforms.
Indeed, it takes courage to love.

The poem "The Courage to Love" is the Author's honest portrayal of the power of love and its effect or impact on people and society.

It is glaringly evident that love is an irresistible influence that opens and closes doors, breaks barriers, fractures understandings, creates and removes obstacles, heals and inflicts, troubles and relieves, betrays and defends, captures and releases, respect and disrespect, kills and saves......we could go on and on but the fact is that we all encounter love and in the end we are either victims or victors.

In spite of this unpredictable nature of love, we still have the courage to love signifying that love has no borders. It encompasses the elements of our thoughts and goes beyond our imaginations.

When Night Falls...

When night falls
that's when you face yourself
family members and friends disappear
walking the beautiful streets no longer matters
the echoes of melodies fail to sate your quest
Oh! When night falls, oblivion consumes the earth

When night falls
and self-imposed walls barricade you
when you weep, scream and can only sob
alone with your unconscious companions
wishing if the walls could only speak
laying bare, revealing the truth
that's when you're forced to face you

When night falls
and the bed fails to accommodate you
the pillows no longer absorb your tears
as fear consumes your every fiber, you know...
Oh! When night falls
you become hopeless
and the journey becomes endless

When night falls
and we are encircled by uncertainties;
persevere! We must remain focus
knowing that it was faith that woke us.
Oh but when rejuvenation unveils itself
and when we are overcome, we realize
Nightfall disappears in a split second

Inspired by: Mrs. Hawa Morgan Tyler, wife of Liberia's Speaker of the House of Representatives. She is a Movie Star, a Composer and Vocalist.

The Author's description of "Night Fall" is a mirror image of the practical experiences we encounter in our respective life journeys. Obviously, everyone has had his or her nightfall, which could simply be financial constraint, serious ailment, joblessness, deeply rooted conflict, barrenness, illiteracy, etc. Though nightfall may vary based on gradation, the Author however presents a turning point in this undesirable journey. This turning point is one's firm commitment to embrace and accommodate perseverance, focus and hope for transformation.

The Misunderstood Child...

The misunderstood child
Your presence is always detested
When your where-about is unknown
Minds are doubtful of your next move
Even when you speak the fact
It sounds unbelievable
Surely, you are misunderstood

Engaging you is forbidden
Even when you are famished
And are fending for crumbs
You are so misinterpreted
When doors are closed before you
You seek endlessly, fetch hopelessly

You are so misread voiceless one
When you are ill, weak, or helpless
or scream and crawl, no one hears or knows
When thirsty, no water to quench your thirst
When hungry, no food to fill your belly
Oh, the misunderstood child

The misunderstood child
The village should be your support
But shamefully you are abandoned
Even your warm smile is unnoticed
Oh child, what a peaceful heart
Oh, What a misunderstood child

The "Misunderstood Child" is the author's realistic description of the paradoxical nature of a person. His or her physical or outward look and inner are in sharp contrast. Born with normal physical structure but somewhere deep inside, there's something quite different that no one knows, sees and feels. His or her inner reality speaks volumes that remain raveled.

Although he or she smiles beamingly but feels unhappy inside, has mouth but hardly afford meal to eat, has ears but doesn't hear, has nose but doesn't smell easily, appears smart but doesn't read and write.

Surely, there's discontentment within thought the outward look portrays a contrary expression. In his or her low self-esteem and lack of assurance for a better future, the expression in the look of this person embodies deceptions. And if we look candidly within ourselves, in spite of our unique physical structures or decent looks, we do carry varying internal struggles and conflicts that portray a misunderstanding which reflect the contradictions and deceptions that characterize our individual life journeys.

Nature is Amazing...

Nature is amazing
in your arms everything exists
good and evil are conceivable
there is peace and there is conflict
the wicked and kind together live
Oh nature, how amazing you are!

Nature is amazing!
Though everything is beautiful
only few are happy or comfortable
Even deep into the rainforest
with unusual companionships
The marauding lion and the antelope
communion together
Truly, Nature you are amazing

Nature is amazing
Where everything seems to be possible
There is sorrow and there is contentment
Success and failure flourish equally
When everyone craves for justice
And the gavel rules eventually
Oh Nature, how amazing is your verdict

Nature is amazing
When the horizon can no longer
hold the sun darkness descends
on the universe
When the moonlight emerges
giving hope to the peasant
Luxury unveils itself to the affluent
Nature, you are indeed amazing

The poem "Nature is Amazing" encapsulates the Author's appreciation of God's astounding creation, its beauty and extensive scope which surpasses human imagination. In spite of the platform nature provides for us to realize the fullness of life, our actions and inactions have created a complete balance between good and evil. Indeed, nature is a place where everything is possible: there's sorrow and there's joy, there's happiness and there's sadness, there's birth and there's death, there's sanity and there's insanity, there's progress and there's backwardness, there's failure and there's success, there's valiant and there's coward, there's perpetrator and there's victim, etc. Truly, Nature is amazing.

Go Home Refugee!

Go home Refugee, Go home
Beyond the horizon from afar
In his shattered motherland
The gun reigns supreme
Its authority unchallenged
With the terrifying echoes
of murder, of rape and of torture
He is consumed by fear
Oh! He would, if he could

Go Home Refugee
In your world of uncertainty
You look on with assured loyalty
But in a shattered world, you feel dejected
Deep inside, you weep and screams silently
And suddenly, the familiar voice resonates
Go home Refugee, Go home.

Go home Refugee
Your humble smile is undesirable
Your afflictions are even so unbearable
In adversity, the day goes by painfully
When famished, you rely only on hope
As the sun disappears from the sky
And darkness shelters your feeble soul
Quietly but audibly, that voice echoes
Go home Refugee, Go home!

From the perspective of the Author, the poem is a reflection of the effects of war on people, especially the consequences of being a Refugee. As a despairing Refugee before, the Author also experienced some of the harsh realities of being a Refugee. Therefore, he was inclined to bring into perspective the need for countries of the world to divert energy, time and resources from war-making to a focus and commitment on improving the livelihood of their people in order to make the world a better place for everyone.

This Peace We Have......

This peace we have
when the sound of the guns
can no longer be heard
and gun barrels are no longer
the source of authority;
When the rich, poor and dejected
can now all fellowship together
This peace should last forever
Oh, how I longed for this peace we have

This peace we have
where the voiceless can now be heard
where citizens no longer live in fear
where the agony of the dagger is gone
and people need no longer shed tears
Oh, how I cherish this peace we have

This peace we have
with reconciliation as our guide
people are moving so fast.
When love and unity transcend hate
peace and stability are assured
Oh, what a blossoming peace we have

This peace we have
when education overcomes illiteracy
progress beats back backwardness
unity supersedes ethnicity
The strong protects the weak and disable
Oh, what a durable and lasting peace we have

This poem was written in commemoration of ten years of uninterrupted peace enjoyed by Liberians following years of civil unrest. The Author's inspiration was drawn from the firm resolve of citizens not to return to conflict.

As a true patriot, the poem is a reflection of the Author's immeasurable contributions to his country's post-conflict recovery efforts and the sustenance of genuine peace in Africa's oldest Republic, Liberia.

Section Two

The following poems deal with a sad period in the history of Liberia-Ebola epidemic. They express briefly the horrors, sorrows, struggles and eventual success in overcoming the EBV epidemic.

The true heroes of the Ebola sagas are the Liberian people who from a community level using a bottom up approach, identified and implemented indigenous solutions to the problem. When the world was shunning the MRU and leaving its citizens to die off, they rose to the task and fought back one of the worse epidemics in modern history.

The story has not been written yet, this is but a footnote in the greater tale but one day, the parts of the Ebola story will all be written. Moreover, when it is, it will be known that the Liberian people were the real heroes.

Of course, we must acknowledge the help of other partners and well-wishers but in the end, it will be known that we as a people overcame our fears, pains, losses and stood as one to conquer EBV at a scale never before experience; at a magnitude no known solution existed.

What a Relationship!

By Joseph N. Boakai, Sr.
Vice President of Liberia

Guinea, Liberia and Sierra Leone
entered into Strange Relationship
with a wicked lady, "Ebola"

She is cunny, comes first as malaria
but later shows her true face

in all of three weeks
she turns on her true color
Running stomach, bloody nose
skin rapture and throwing-up
in disgrace with

She has misinterpreted God's intent
For marriage-till death do us part
She makes sure you go together

She is not easy to divorce
Don't go to Church,
she kills the Pastor
Go to the Doctor and make sure
You don't compromise your health
Get rid of her at all cost

Never in the history of Liberia has the country been so devastated by a health calamity such as the Ebola Virus Disease (EVD). When the deadly virus engulfed our dear country, it inflicted pain and agony on the already war-wearied and impoverished people. With determination, the scourge attacked and killed thousands of innocent Liberians. It tore families apart and further devastated an already weak and unstable economy. It set the people against each other on one hand, and against their government on the other hand. Like her neighbors Sierra Leone and Guinea, this seed of discord kept Liberia in isolation once again bringing back the horrible memories of the fourteen-year civil crisis. Indeed, citizens were not only consumed by fear and apprehensions but became hopeless and eventually lost the courage to confront this common enemy... But not all was lost. With the determination, fortitude and efforts of the citizens combined, a common front was in sight. Human and financial resources, communities and organizations were mobilized and with faith and perseverance, Ebola has been defeated.

These poems do not only reflect the author's immeasurable contributions to the fight against the Ebola Virus Disease but a clear manifestation of how a united people with a common goal can surmount a challenge of any sort or degree.

Ebola, the Invisible Killer

Oh Ebola, you are invisible and deadly
You roam the world like an evil spirit
You have no specific target
Destroying the provider and the dependent
Sentencing them to death unjustly
Casting fear and despair
Ebola, you are an invisible killer

Your reign is undesirable
For you are worse than war
In your heartlessness
You shoot your silent gun
Devouring your blameless victim
Your presence is forever forbidden
Oh Ebola, you are merciless

In your cowardice
You creep on the poor and the rich
Manifesting your shameful prowess
Destroying the fabric of societies
Yet, as invisible as you are
You are not invincible

Ebola, you are demystified
Your reign is in crisis
Your time is up
With courage, faith and perseverance
You will soon become history
And our land will be free

Ebola, Our Common Enemy

Oh Ebola, you're a seed of discord
You kill the rich and the poor
Tearing families and nations apart
Breaking relationships and breeding animosity
You have no borderlines
In your covertness, you are strongly rejected
Ebola, you are our common enemy

Maintaining your agenda of backwardness
You disrupt and undermine progress
Destroying economies and solidarities
Ebola, you have no conscience
In your silent brutality
You inflict pain and suffering
Oh Ebola, this cruelty must stop

The final battle lines are drawn
You now face a whole nation
A united army ready for battle
Firm with a common purpose
To pursue and destroy you
Courageous and determined
Ebola, the battle is irreversible

Ebola, Your Time is Up!

You come like a thief in the night
Creeping in deep silence
Evading every semblance of light
With your wicked intent
You use your merciless claws
To infect and destroy your innocent prey
Ebola, your time is up

Ebola, you waged your invisible war
Massively taking the lives of vulnerable people
With your shameful virulence
You ravaged their nations
In their state of confusion and weakness
You displayed your cruelty
Surely, your time is up

Ebola, your time is up
In your so-called battle
Your mysteries have been unraveled
And your weakness exposed
With courage and determination
The end of your terror is in sight
Indeed, your time is up

About the Author

The author is an administrator, educator and development practitioner with more than twelve years of professional experience in the public sector particularly, in the areas of education management, democracy and governance in Liberia. He has authored three books and several published articles. The Author holds a Bachelor of Arts degree in Political Science with emphasis on International Relations from the University of Liberia and is a candidate for Master of Arts Degree in Peace Studies and Conflict Transformation at the Kofi Annan Institute for Conflict Transformation at the University of Liberia. The Author is a proud recipient of the ALLIA/ADLA 2015 award for outstanding services.

Other Books

- Essential Elements for Liberia's Post-Conflict Recovery

- Emergence of Democratic Governance in Liberia: Challenges and Prospects Feb 4, 2015

- From Refugee to Prominence: A Memoire

Featured in this anthology

- Portor Portor: 12 New African Poets